SEO

The Seven Tips to Succeed in Google

THOMAS CLAYTON

Copyright © 2016 Franky | studio

All rights reserved.

ISBN: 1533341710
ISBN-13: 978-1533341716

Table of Contents

Introduction

I want to thank you and congratulate you for purchasing *SEO: The Seven Tips to Succeed in Google*. Search engine optimization is a crucial part of managing a successful website and purchasing this book and others like it is the first step towards making the most of the opportunity. It is important to move forward with realistic expectations, however, your search engine rankings will not improve overnight. With hard work and dedication, you can certainly expect to see results sooner than later.

This book contains proven steps and strategies designed to ensure you have everything you need to improve your SEO across the board. It starts with choosing the right keywords before moving on to optimizing your website to its fullest including the meta tags and the types of content you are producing. Follow the tips suggested in the chapters included here and you will soon see real, measurable success when it comes to improving your Google search ranking. With enough work you may even eventually reach rank number 1.

Thanks again for purchasing this book, I hope you enjoy it!

Chapter 1: Understanding SEO

Search Engine Optimization (SEO) is increasingly becoming a more integral part of any business's marketing strategy as easy visibility from a basic Google or Bing search remains the simplest and most effective way to draw in new customers. SEO can be difficult for those running a small business to begin using without some prior training as there are several different facets required to use them effectively. For example, SEO is just as much about what content you use to populate your site as it is about the way your entire website is structured.

While other means, including having an active social media presence, will help to generate some additional traffic for your site, they are much more effective when used as a way that maximizes SEO at the same time. As such, it is important to take the time to ensure that the content from your website, as well as the website itself, is as readily available to the relevant databases as possible. While this process may seem difficult and time consuming at first, the results will always far outweigh the costs. What's more, improving your SEO is free marketing, not committing to it fully is akin to leaving money on the table.

Search engines like Google or Bing work by sending out automated programs known as crawlers which follow links in URLs to every page that is currently active online. The crawlers then store relevant information from each page in databases that then return that information to users as search results. As you might expect, parsing all of this data in a matter of a few seconds requires some serious filtering which is where keywords initially came from.

As the internet grew in popularity, however, a simple keyword search was no longer enough and now there are numerous other factors included such as site descriptions and popularity to ensure that users always receive the most useful search results possible. This is what makes SEO so crucial as not succeeding in all areas can often be akin to not succeeding at all as your site will be passed over by sites who are firing on all cylinders.

This is why common terms that potential clients use when searching for good and services each carry extraordinary value, targeting the right type of traffic at the right time can make the difference between success and failure for even a business that is otherwise at least moderately successful. What's worse, filling in the appropriate boxes with the wrong content can burry your otherwise completely competent website amongst unrelated searches where literally no one will ever find it. The early days of the Internet are behind us, the digital space is just as cutthroat as any other marketplace, it is important that you respond in kind.

While SEO is an incredibly complicated subject that is often hotly debated, the good news is that with a little bit of hard work and studying, you can get a majority of the benefits of hiring an SEO manager by yourself. While you won't necessarily be leading the pack when it comes to online content, you will at least be in the running.

When it comes to learning SEO, the biggest cost will be the time commitment that you decide improving your website's SEO is worth.

Even if you ultimately decide to hand the process over to someone else, the tips in the following chapters will still help you make the most of any contributions you do make to the process. Consider the tips in the following chapters and, with a little practice, you will be able to keep your head above water in the ever changing ocean that is SEO.

SEO: How to Get On the First Page of Google

Chapter 2: Find the Right Keywords

When it comes to choosing the keywords that best define your website, you are most likely thinking in terms of pure SEO, the best keywords go beyond this, however, and reflect how the company or website pictures itself at the most basic level. Consider the following suggestions when it comes to choosing the keywords that define your site, and whatever you do, don't make your final decision lightly.

Keywords are becoming key phrases: As the internet has grown, the singular keyword has been replaced with multiple keywords but even that seems as though it is no longer enough which is why key phrases are currently becoming more and more common. While it can be easy to overthink choosing your key phrases, the key to finding the right balance is to be neither too broad nor too specific. For example, if your website sells nutritionally conscious dog food, then on their own the words food and dog will not get you where you need to be. Instead, a better choice would be to choose words that relate to the specialty ingredients your dog foods contain.

The most effective key phrases tend to be between 2 and 4 words that encompass your website in the most common terminology possible. Single words should always be avoided as they tend to be both general and competitive, neither of which will prove terribly effective when it comes to improving your site ranking.

It is best to do some research as sometimes common phrases that seem as though they would be used in regards to specific types of content are actually quite unpopular. The fewer search results you find returned when you search for a phrase, the less popular that phrase is with the public. Again, your ultimate goal should be to find a phrase that perfectly bridges the gap between competitively popular and completely ineffective. Remember, work to attract people who want to interact with your page, not simply meaningless page views.

Refrain from making keywords a contest: Depending on the type of website you are interested in promoting, it may be tempting to include what are known as vanity keywords, that is, words that are included in the keywords section solely to see who can be king or queen of that particular search. While finding yourself at the top of that particular search can provide an ego boost, the odds of it happening are rarely in favor of anyone other than major corporations or sites that include the keyword in their name. It is therefore almost always better to go with something more precisely tailored to your business while still being a reasonable thing for someone to type into a search engine.

Repeat keywords as needed: While the value of repeating keywords is frequently debated, it turns out that efficacy is more important than simple repetition. Repeating virtual identical words or phrases results in minimal additional gain while repeating relevant words in useful contexts tends to yield more reliable results. Rather than cramming multiple related keywords onto a single page, a more effective approach would be to instead split the topics up across multiple pages, giving users a better chance to return options to each. When it comes to SEO, a broad net is frequently the best option.

Always have an SEO strategy in mind: Whenever you go to create new content for your site, which ideally should be multiple times per day as freshness of content also factors into search results, it is important to do so with a clear idea of what keywords you are going to tag the content with before it goes live. Having a firm outline of what you will need to include in the content in order for the keywords to be relevant will make it easier to determine what you will need to write to make it so.

Chapter 3: Optimize Your Website

Once you have a handle on the right types of keywords, it is important to take a critical look at your website and determine if you are doing everything in your power to make your site as efficient as possible when it comes to maximizing SEO.

Consider the speed at which your website loads: In a world that increasingly relies on smaller devices to return real-time results, the length of time that your website loads can literally make the difference between a successful interaction and a failed one. Likewise, it is important to ensure that everything that appears on the traditional version of your website appears properly when viewed on a mobile platform. Ensure that form never supersedes function when it comes to presenting your website and you will already be going a long way towards improving your search ranking. Remember, if people can't see you site in as many places as possible, your ranking will suffer, it is as simple as that.

Take the time to think about user behavior signals: These days, Google is giving more and more weight to the experience that users have while visiting particular sites, including things such as number of ads that are immediately visible and ease of use when it comes to navigation with the goal of making results as pleasing to users as possible. This means that is important to ensure that users engage with your site as much as possible, but only in positive ways.

To ensure that these interactions are as smooth as possible, it is important to start with a fully-featured and useful search function. Studies show that as many as 90 percent of all website interactions start with the use of a search function which means that if yours is not up to snuff, you are likely to lose users before they even begin to really interact with your site in a meaningful manner.

Along those same lines, it is important to ensure that all the links on your site work properly, as broken links decay visitor confidence and literally prevent them from interacting with your site any further. In general, having the proper type of internal linking structure (articles that link to other articles) will improve the number of pages that the average visitor views on your site and will make them more likely to return again in the future as well. In addition, articles that link to multiple other articles which all include a particular set of keywords are more likely to show up on those types of searches.

It is also important that all of your URLs use easily decipherable words and not long strings of text. Lots of internal links that are clearly legible will allow crawlers to view your site more easily and the longer they spend on internal links the more trustworthy your website will appear.

Don't forget about images: When it comes to optimizing your website, it is just as important to add appropriate and relevant data to your pictures as it is to any other part of your site. A picture is worth a thousand words, add full descriptions for each and you'll have more ways to link relevant data to your site.

Keep headlines short: Headlines for your articles should appear in all of your permalinks to the content which means they should contain no more than 54 characters which is the max that is visible per result on the resulting page that appears after a search has been performed. Shorter permalinks are also easier for crawlers to parse which makes them more effective in that regard as well. When it comes to setting permalinks, don't be afraid to include keywords as well as Google will recognize 4 keywords per permalink URL.

Don't underestimate comments: Having a vibrant and active community comment section frequently requires a time commit to moderate properly, this is often worth it, however, as the additional interaction that people will have with your site, and your ultimate search ranking will more than make up for the difference.

Chapter 4: Maximize Social Media

In this day and age, having a powerful social media presence is practically a requirement for running a successful website, assuming you already a robust social media presence, there are several things you can do to parley that into successful SEO.

Start by focusing on your followers: The more people that are linked to your social media profile, the more weight that profile will have when it comes to search engine ranking. While these things don't outrank things like quality of content, social media does provide a bonus to overall ranking and should not be ignored when it comes to making attempts to improve search engine rankings. Websites and brands that have a large number of followers are thought of in more positive terms by unaffiliated consumers under the traditional wisdom that so many people can't be wrong. It is important to keep this mindset at the forefront of your motivation when it comes to working hard to improve your website's social media presence; as this can be difficult to initially get off the ground in many situations.

This doesn't mean that you should simply spam visitors for their social media information, however, as the quality of the interactions with these followers is rated as well. It is more effective to have 10,000 involved followers than it is to have 100,000 bots and otherwise disengaged followers. As long as you are persistent in your goal to attract new followers and consistent when it comes to regularly creating additional content, then there is no reason that your followers should not continue to grow over time. Remember, attracting social media followers is a marathon, not a sprint, slow and steady wins the race.

Link, link, link

The more websites that link to pages on your website, the more weight your website will be given when it comes to ranking considerations. A vast array of different external links that appear as a result of a successful social media post will cause that post to have additional authority in Google's eyes. Get a few posts that are seen as having lots of authority and you will find your overall site ranking more likely to climb regularly. For more on creating the right type of content to encourage additional linking, see chapter 6.

Increasing your SEO effectives is all about increasing your apparent level of authority and for every 1,000 shares, retweets and replies that your links turn up in, your search ranking increases just a little bit. Make this into a habit and you will see real results in terms of improving your ranking, though it is unreasonable to assume they will happen overnight. In order to make this type of thing more common, take the time to engage with visitors to your sight directly. Offering incentives for those who share links to your posts with several of their friends is a great way for visitors to get into the habit of doing so, even when incentives are not available.

Surveys or quizzes are also great for spawning shares naturally as long as the results are easily linkable. Posting these types of things regularly will naturally cause people to share their results if they catch on with a particular community. The best part of this strategy is the fact that it perpetuates itself without additional effort on your end. Visitors posting their results will cause new followers who will be drawn in who will then repeat the process indefinably assuming the content remains evergreen.

Chapter 5: Consider External Tools

While there are lots of details to consider when it comes to using SEO effectively, the good news is that you don't have to worry about doing it all by yourself, even when you are trying to go it alone. Consider the following free SEO enhancement tools when it comes to making the most of your current push towards SEO success.

PageSpeed Insights by Google: Available from a quick Google search, this website allows you to enter your website and get back a real time loading and performance analysis for both mobile and standard versions of the site. It also includes a general user experience score including things like legible fonts, content size, ease of tapping and more. If you are interested in maximizing your website in every way possible, this is a great place to start.

Local Listing by Moz: Available at Moz.com, this is a great resource for those with brick and mortar locations, as well as websites, as it searches through a variety of different data bases including search engines and social media sites to determine how it compares to other local similar businesses in the area. It also includes suggestions on how to finish filling out listings that might otherwise remain incomplete.

The Keyword Tool: Available at KeyWordTool.io this site allows you to enter in any keyword and provides you with a list of more relevant key phrases to use instead. If you are adding keywords to your site for the first time and aren't sure where to start, the keyword tool is a logical choice.

Keyword Planner by Google: Available at AdWords.Google.com, this tool allows you to put in any keyword or phrase to show how many times it has been used in the past month. It also displays the amount of competition currently surrounding that particular word or phrase and also suggests alternatives that are in the desired level of competition and frequency. If you are having trouble narrowing down the right keywords for your website, this resource should be considered invaluable.

Trends from Google: Available at Google.com/trends, this tool will allow you to enter a specific term or topic to see how frequently that topic has been searched in the past week, month or even year, as well as to project estimated trends for the future. If you are looking to get in on a keyword or phrase on the ground floor, this is a logical place to start.

Webmaster Tools for Google: A simple search will bring you to the page for a variety of webmaster tools that will provide you with a complete overview of how the search engine sees your site as it currently is. It will provide you with an in-depth view of your site that will allow for any indexing issues, alerts or bugs to come to light. This site does require a plugin be added to your site, the specifics of which vary depending on the type of site you use.

Site Explorer: The site explorer is available from Moz.com and can scan your site to determine which links you use most frequently as well as which links are used the most both for traffic coming to and leaving your site. This is a great way to determine which types of social media seem to be most effective in driving traffic to your site so you can focus future efforts in the area in which they will do the most good. When it comes to sites that you link to frequently, consider contacting the other site and setting up a more formal affiliate connection if appropriate, additional visibility will allow the flow of links to go both directions.

SimilarWeb: Available at SimilarWeb.com, this website allows you to compare any two websites, for example yours and that of your primary competitor, in categories such as social media presence, search traffic, referrals, SEO and more.

Chapter 6: Create the Right Type of Content

When it comes to ensuring that the content you are creating is the content people are interested in, there are no surefire methods for success beyond the obvious. That is, write quality engaging content and people will respond to it. Here are a few pointers to steer you in the right direction.

Use longer form content: While at one point, writing articles that included lots of clunky keywords was the best way to get attention from search engines. These days, recent studies show that sites that contain longer form content that focuses on improving the reader's experience tend to rank higher than those that post shorter, choppier content. The end result here is that if you take the time to consider what your visitors are looking for, and then provide them with that information, your search engine ranking will respond in kind.

Specifically, statistically speaking, a majority of results that are ranked number 1 in their respective categories tended to have slightly less than 2,500 words per page. The entry ranked number 2 tended to be slightly longer and the length decreases in relation to the ranking from there. The message here is clear, people are looking for explanations of concepts and ideas that are long enough to be thorough, but short enough to not require an extended commitment to benefit from. Use this to your advantage and choose the length of your content appropriately.

Choose the right audience: When it comes to deciding who you are creating content for, you can either choose the complete novice, the expert, or someone in-between. When it comes to choosing an audience that will lead to the greatest overall boost to your SEO, targeting an audience who would appreciate a refresher on the basics but are also interested in some more detail is generally the best choice. Experts are often difficult to please and novices might not know what they want, someone on just the other side of beginner, however, is the most likely to stick around. Writing with the goal of somewhere just to the left of the middle allows you to bring in some novices as well as the occasional expert looking for a refresher.

Consider formatting: Even if you are providing the best content on a specific topic imaginable, if your website looks outdated, unprofessional or is otherwise difficult to read, either in mobile or traditional formats, then you are likely to lose visitors' interest before you've even had a chance to capture it properly. One of the biggest offenders of this type are pages that are nothing but walls of text. If your website looks like a textbook, you'll turn off new visitors guaranteed.

While pictures that add value to the content they are breaking up and spacing out are better, stock photos still serve the function of ensuring that your website looks like it was created this decade and their importance cannot be overstated. If you are having difficulty finding relevant pictures, consider comics or other cartoons, stock photos or charts and graphs. Personalized pictures, especially those that are then posted to social media separately tend to create the most response from potential followers and should be used whenever possible, especially when first building your online presence.

Be authoritative: Whatever your writing about, it is important for readers to feel as though they can trust the information that you are presenting. If you don't have the type of qualifications that automatically generate the desired level of authority, it is important to always cite sources in your posts or to otherwise quote people who are experts in specific fields. This doesn't mean plagiarize quotes from other sources, track down the original material or give other sites credit where credit is due.

Chapter 7: Understand Available Metadata

Metadata tags are similar to keywords and phrases in that they make it easier for your pages to show up in the appropriate search results. Unlike keywords, they do not naturally show up on the pages themselves and instead are only visible in the code that is used to create the particular page in question. Consider metadata tags the keywords for the data about the data.

You can see the meta tags of any page by right clicking on it and selecting the view page source option. The meta tag specifics will be found near the top of the screen. Meta tags can be altered by anyone with a basic understanding of HTML, or, from the appropriate menu option from the backend of your website.

There are four types of meta tags that are useful when it comes to improving your SEO; meta attribute keywords are keywords related to the current page, the title tag is the title that search engines display when the page is referenced and the meta attribute description is the brief description of the page that comes up when the page is referenced as a search result. Finally, the meta attribute robots is used to tell crawlers how to interact with the page.

Keywords attribute: Due to the prevalence of keyword stuffing over the years, the keywords attribute is utilized less frequently than it was in the past. As such, it is a useful tool to use for its intended purpose as it will give you a small SEO bump compared to sites that don't bother to utilize them to their full potential.

Title Tag: This is the currently reigning king of meta tags which is why it is important to ensure that yours are formatted properly every single time. This tag also appears at the top of the page in question as its title so it can be seen by every visitor to your site as well. It is important to choose a title tag that clearly indicates what the page in question contains while still including at least one or two key words or phrases if possible. This is the title that will appear in all search engine results moving forward, make it a good one.

Description Attribute: When you aren't the number 1 result on a specific type of search, the description attribute is the attribute that is most likely to sway uncertain potential visitors in one direction or another. This is the description that will tell Google what your page is about, it is important to include as much relevant truthful information in this scenario as possible. It is also important to be as brief as possible as you have about 20 words to get your message across effectively.

Always include as many relevant keywords or phrases in this section as possible. While the keywords used in this attribute won't directly influence your SEO ranking, studies show that seeing the keywords they were looking for in the description makes potential visitors much more likely to choose one website over another. Think of this space as free advertising as to the benefits of coming to your page as opposed to any other page in all of digital space.

Robot Attribute: The robot attribute is perhaps the most straightforward of all of the modifiable attributes as there are only two options you can choose from. The index/noindex option tells various search engines whether or not you want your page to be returned from basic search results. The follow/nofollow option on the other hand tells crawlers whether or not they are supposed to follow links on your pages to their destinations or not. In most instances, you should choose index and follow respectively.

Chapter 8: Maximize Local SEO

With the ever increasing number of search results available to any given query, many Internet users are prioritizing results that are in a close proximity to their homes as a way of separating the virtual wheat from the digital chaff. Taking the time to focus, not just on general SEO but, local SEO as well will provide you with an edge over much of your competition.

Be consistent: To increase your chances of appearing in the initial round of Google Maps listings for a specific search result, the first thing you need to do is to ensure that your business is listed with its phone number, address, name and website readily available in all the common online listing sites in your area. While this seems as though it would be common knowledge, recent studies confirm that as many as 80 percent of small businesses have a disparity of information when it comes to one or more of these listing sites. Forewarned is forearmed, however, don't be like the majority, make it as easy for customers to contact you as possible.

There is nothing that will kill a potential customer's enthusiasm for your business faster than inaccurate information. The more people refer to your website through these listing sites, the more likely you are to move up the Goggle Map results. Do yourself a favor and ensure that everything listed for your business is right, every time. In order to appear on Google Maps, every point of data between what the customer types in and what is listed for your business must match up, do your part to ensure all of this information is accurate.

Focus on social media: More so than even traditional SEO, local SEO thrives on the connections that social media provides. With the right social media approach, local business stop being seen as such and start being seen as real people. Customers are much more likely to frequent stores where they feel as though their contributions matter and social media is a great first step.

Small businesses tend to thrive when they give back to the community they are a part of and social media can play a big part in this interaction as well. Get out there and get connected and you will be surprised at the direct correlation between increase your social media following and increasing your business. Having an active online community means your search result will be rated higher, contain customer reviews and plenty of 5 star ratings; these people aren't rating a business, they are helping out a member of their community.

Depending on the content and functionality of your website, it is common for many people to view the social media page for their favorite local businesses as their primary point of contact, traditional website or no. If you find yourself in this type of situation, instead of trying to drive traffic from one to the other, simply post additional relevant information on your social media page instead. Whether it is Facebook, Twitter, Instagram or even YouTube, if you can find an engaged audience, it is best to make the most of it while you can. Remember to always remain engaged and to show the community that you appreciate them as well.

What's more, active communities tend to branch out and leave local reviews on websites such as Yelp.com. It is important to cater to these types of reviewers whenever possible as every Yelp review will show up separately on a standard Google search. This fact can either work in your advantage if you have pages and pages of good reviews, or work against you if those reviews are unilaterally negative.

Conclusion

Thank you again for purchasing this book! I hope it was able to help you learn everything there is to know about maximizing your search engine optimization potential across all possible avenues. With the amount of new content constantly being generated online it can seem as though breaking through the continuous stream with anything worthwhile on a reliable basis is nearly impossible. This could not be further from the truth, however, and with enough hard work and perseverance you will eventually find that you have complete mastery over several keywords and phrases.

The next step is to stop reading and start optimizing your website to ensure maximum SEO effectiveness in as many ways as possible. Don't be discouraged if you don't see immediate results, eventually dividends will appear. Above all, it is important to keep at it every single day, your competition certainly is.

Finally, if you enjoyed this book, then I'd like to ask you for a favor, would you be kind enough to leave a review for this book on Amazon? It'd be greatly appreciated!

Glossary of Terms

Throughout this book, you have seen some SEO related terms that will be explained in this addendum.

Anchor Text: a keyword or phrase used to hyperlink an internal or external webpage to your site.

Backlink: an external link that links from an outside source such as social media back to your website.

Blacklist: a list of websites that are never going to appear in Google search results due to a flagrant disregard for Google search engine rules. Otherwise considered the black hole of websites.

eCommerce: online retail locations, typically selling products, and not services.

External Link: a link that takes a person from your website to another website or links back to your site from a different website.

Google AdWords: Google's keyword search program designed for pay per click and banner ads, but can be used to generate keyword lists.

Google Analytics: Google's statistical report app that can be attached to your website, or accessed through Google Webmaster Tools, where you can study visitor reports and page ranking results.

Hyperlink: a link to a specific keyword, where you can click on the word or phrase and be taken to a new page on the website.

Internal Link: A link on your website that takes a person from page to page in your site, which can be from the homepage to a product page, like a hyperlink.

SEO: short for search engine optimization, which is the tactics used to design your website for optimal search results, i.e. the strategy you employ to get a top rank in search results based on keywords and other practices.

Search Engine Bot: a "robot.txt" that searches webpages and websites to index the pages for better search results.

Spider: Also known as crawlers, bots, and Google bots, spiders crawl through webpages to rank the page for relevance based on category and search criteria.

WordPress: A blogging website with free, personal, and professional websites designed for blogging, portfolios, eCommerce, and other styles of websites.

Here you will find the tools used by me!

New Article Submitter Software - Submit To 668 Directories!

Seopressor Wordpress SEO Plugin, Better, Faster, Higher Ranking!

Traffic Travis Free SEO And PPC Software

Backlink Beast - Best SEO Software

EXTRA

Fast Memorization Techniques:
Accelerated Learning - Advanced Technique for Fast Learning

JOE BRONSKI

Disclaimer

Introduction

Have you ever wondered what the difference between you and someone who seems to able to endlessly spout facts they have memorized? Or while you were in school why others just seemed to have a much easier time remember facts for tests or were always getting better scores then you? Though some people are just naturally gifted learners the odds are they were taught techniques you were not exposed to and has given them the ability to better retain the information they were taught. They also most likely practiced their techniques keeping their mind sharp and making retention all the easier for their efforts.

There are so many techniques out there for memorization and learning. Some are more effective then others and they all depend on the type of learner you are. This book has been put together to help cover some of the more advanced memorization techniques that can be utilized. Most learning is considered the tradition approach with the student in a more passive role and the teacher will actively put knowledge before the student in an attempt to help them retain the information.

While this has had some success in the past, research has revealed that an accelerated learning approach helps a learner retain more information faster than the tradition techniques. This style encourages the student to become an active participant in their learning as well as helping them truly manipulate the material allowing for total retention in a shorter timeframe. It also allows them to have a much greater grasp of the material because they are forced to place it in their own words and manipulate the information in a way that allows their brain to better understand the concepts they are learning.

This book will go over these techniques in some detail in the hope of helping you become faster and more efficient at memorizing important information. There are different aspects of material that help to determine how difficult it is to study. Theses properties will be discussed as well as strategies that can be used to improve how effectively you can memorize those types of material. We will discuss ways in which you can properly prepare your body for memorization and give you the best chances at retaining the information. It is also believed that seeking a few other sources before you begin your studying can help you give a broader picture and better understanding of what your learning.

Hopefully with the information you are given here, you will be able to efficiently and more completely memorize information that you need to retain. Remember working with your mind is just like working any other muscle in your body. You need to consistently work with it to strengthen the muscle. By applying some of these techniques as well as practicing everyday just like you would if you were an athlete you will be able to better improve your abilities to memorize and retain.

Chapter 1: Why Memorization is Difficult and How to Help Yourself

With research it has been determined that there are about 11 characteristics of information that determine how difficult or easy something is to memorize. Armed with the knowledge of these various characteristics you will hopefully be able to identify why certain knowledge it easier to retain while you struggle in other areas. After you have been given these characteristics will go over strategies that can help you improve memorization with information containing the various characteristics.

- ✓ Abstractness, this characteristic refers to how easy it is to wrap your head around the concept. If the concept is abstract in a nature it will be harder to relate to and make it all the more difficult to put into terms that you will be able to easily understand. The harder an object is to understand the more difficult it is to remember.

- ✓ Complexity, how complex or difficult a problem is can certainly determine how difficult it can be to retain. The more intricate the information the harder it will be for your mind to remember everything in its proper place.

- ✓ Familiarity, is how much exposure you have had to the information you are trying to retain. If you are memorizing information on something you interact with on a day to day basis it will be easier to remember information about it.

- ✓ Humanness, this characteristic refers to how relatable a subject is to the human experiences in life. The more relevance a subject has to being human or experiences we face as human beings the easier it is to relate to and retain.

- ✓ Immediacy, how soon information needs to be retained. The shorter the time frame that information needs to be memorized by the harder or easier it can be to retain depending on your personality.

✓ Importance, this characteristic points to how much the information you are trying to memorize impacts your life. The more important it can be to your life in any way can make it easier to remember.

✓ Order, the more logical the structure of the information the easier it will be to retain. The more convoluted the information and the harder to decipher its proper order the more difficult it will be for you to remember. Our minds immediately seek to make things easier for us to understand, so if the order doesn't make sense it will be harder for our brains to retain.

✓ Relevance, the more useful information will be to you the easier it will be to retain. If its something you can use in your everyday life or can help you in your endeavors the odds are it will be easier to memorize.

✓ Salience, when we find information boring it makes it that much harder to focus on the subject. When your bored in class you fall asleep, a similar thing can happen to your brain. When it's bored it can fall asleep in a sense and make it more difficult to retain what your attempting to.

✓ Sensuous, how your senses receive the information you want to learn will help to determine how much easier it is to retain. If you can sense it on more planes it is more likely you will be able to remember it.

✓ Size, this characteristic can easily be seen as one that helps determine your retention of something. The more their is to retain the more difficult it can be.

Now that we have talked about how these characteristics affect how easy or hard it can be to retain information we will go over ways in which you can improve in areas you might struggle in. If you add characteristics to the material you are trying to retain and you discover a pattern to the types of material you struggle with then you can use these tips to hopefully help you overcome your shortcomings in that retention area.

✓ Abstractness, try to relate the information to what's around you. If you can find a way to make it less abstract and easier to relate to the everyday it will be that much easier to remember.

✓ Complexity, if you break it down into smaller pieces or simpler steps it can make it easier to understand and retain.

✓ Familiarity, try to review information more frequently. If you can try to review it for a short amount of time every day. The more you are exposed to it the more familiar you will be with it.

✓ Humanness, turn your information in a story and try to make yourself the main character. Not only will it help you relate the information to something more natural. By making yourself the star it will be all the more interesting to remember.

✓ Immediacy, setting yourself a deadline to have information retained by can help keep you motivated even if you don't need it for any particular time. Sometimes if you don't need it for a test or something similar you may procrastinate on the material in question.

- ✓ Importance, try to set a goal or objective to memorizing the information. If you can make it more important to yourself, it will be easier to retain.

- ✓ Order, if you struggle to remember information and the order makes no sense simply restructure it in a way that makes sense to you. You will then be able to better retain the information.

- ✓ Relevance, if you figure out a way in which it can be relevant to your life it will make it easier to retain.

- ✓ Salience, try to create a story to go along with the information. If you can string the information together in a funny or crazy way it will not only be more memorable but it will keep it more interesting.

- ✓ Sensuous, if you can only associate your information with one sense you may find it harder to retain but if you try to find other sense that it can relate to you will find it easier to remember. It may take a little creativity to figure out how to engage other senses but it can be a big help.

- ✓ Size, if you have a large amount of material to cover break it down into smaller chunks to give your brain a more manageable chunk of information to remember.

When memorizing information most people use familiarity in order to retain information. Others who are better at retaining information.

Chapter 2: Preparing Your Body

One of the most important things you can do to help you become a memorization wiz is to take care of yourself. By ensuring that your system is running at its best you will give your mind the best shot possible to retain information. A body that is sleep deprived or not given the proper fuel will not function as well as one that is. So by following a few of these simple steps you will set your mind up for success and making learning and retaining what you have learned that much easier.

Get enough sleep, it cannot be stressed enough how important sleep is. Try to get at least 7 hours of sleep a day, a well rested mind is more prepared to retain information and is just more ready to work in general. Also minimize your blue light exposure before going to sleep, so avoid computers, your phones, and TV before bed.

Try to keep yourself well hydrated. If you can keep water or maybe even some unsweetened tea, sugar will defeat the exercise, your body and brain will be able to better function getting the water that it needs to live off of.

Sugar can be your enemy in the case of studying, it may seem like a great jolt to keep you going but the crash can stop you in your tracks and make things worse for you. The excess energy can be the wrong kind making your more fidgety then able to sit and focus like you may need to.

Walk or exercise on a regular basis if you can. The better your body function the healthier you will feel and your brain will feel. You are also more likely to feel happier and better about yourself and this lift in mood can make focusing and studying that much easier.

Try to avoid stressors and schedule out your day to a certain degree so you can reach optimal productivity during your day. Not only will you feel like you have accomplished something it will help keep you from stressing about things you need to accomplish because you will already be preparing your brain.

Chapter 3: A Few Other Techniques

In this day and age there are far too many distractions available to take our attention away from the tasks at hand. But if you would like to be able to memorize information faster and become a better learner there are a few techniques you can employ to help you double or even triple the amount of information you can retain in your sessions. When you allow yourself to be distracted you make it that much harder for your brain to simple take in the information you are presenting it. With those other distractions joking for the position of attention in your mind it will force you to work that much harder to try and remember.

If you are a music lover try to listen to music without lyrics. Music with lyrics can interfere with your language processing abilities. So when you listen to music with lots of lyrics you're essentially sabotaging yourself. Your brain will be unable to totally focus on one set of information because the other will either be spoken or read and disrupt the flow of the other. So instead try to listen to music that is only instrumental. If you can stay away from music that has any lyrics your can still listen to sounds in the background without distracting yourself from the material and make learning and retention that much easier.

Try to choose times that are most conducive to studying. If you choose to work when you are very likely to be interrupted, you will easily be distracted with each interruption and make it that much harder for yourself. Also shoot for times with your have energy. If you are tired your mind is likely to be clear and able to engage in the types of mental gymnastics you are asking of it. You would never ask you body to run a marathon when you are exhausted so why ask the same of your brain? It is a muscle too. By keeping distractions to a minimum and being properly energized you are also less likely to experience stress while studying which can also make it easier on yourself. The more stressed you are the harder it will be to concentrate on the task at hand.

With the technology available to us it can be extremely hard to disconnect from everything and everyone around us. By having a cellphone, you are totally accessible to everyone at all times. This constant connection can be so distracting, talking with your friends or finding out what someone just posted on Facebook can be so much more engaging then the studying you are trying to accomplish. But if you want to be able to memorize and retain the information you are working with you need to do yourself a favor and unplug from everything around you. Turn off notifications, your cell phone, whatever you need to do to be totally focused on the task at hand. This can be very hard for some people especially if they have never done it before. If this is the case for you try for about 20 minutes at a time. You don't want to drive yourself to distraction by being unplugged because that wont achieve anything either.

Many people studying sitting or laying down. While this restful state can help keep you focused on one thing and one thing only you also don't want to completely sit like a lump the whole time. Standing and walking around for short breaks can help promote blood flow and even energy into your body. Both are helpful for keeping you fresh and focused. You also provide more oxygen to your brain from the increased blood flow and the more oxygen your brain has the better it will function.

Prioritize the material you are about to review. If say you feel very confident on certain parts of the information you are cover then you should skip those parts and review what you are shakier with. When you go over material you are already very familiar with you can give yourself a false sense of security. You will feel like you know more and take time away from the information that really needs your attention. It will also increase your exposure to what you are unfamiliar with helping you to each maximum retention of all the topics you are trying to remember.

Tell yourself a story. This is one that can't be stressed enough, if you can find a story to help show you the information you are trying to learn that's excellent and you should read it. But if you can make one up, by placing information into a relatable story your brain will have an easier time remember that then trying to chock down random bits of information. Telling your story to someone else or even attempting to teach them material will also help you to better retain it. When you teach someone else you are forced to reword the information and put it into each to understand bites for someone who doesn't know the material. This rewording and forcing you to really work with the concepts will give you a better understanding and make it that much easier to understand.

The last tip to keep in mind is to try and preview the content you are about to go over. By going on other websites or searching in other books before getting down to some serious studying or memorization you can help to give yourself perspective on material that might not necessarily be clear from the source you are currently reading. It can make things clearer it can also give you different perspective that can help the information to click in your mind and help you to remember it better. You can also give yourself a bigger picture if you skim before you read in detail. You will better be able to see where the text is heading and hopefully by causing that light of recognition in your brain you will be reinforcing some pathways in your brain.

Conclusion

Thank you for purchasing this book. There is a lot of information out there just waiting to be retained for you to use later or apply to your everyday life. So why would you want to wait or let everything that there is to learn out their pass you by? The world is full of so much knowledge and now with some of the techniques in this book anyone can start memorizing information like a pro.

Try to work through all the techniques in this book and don't forget about a few life style changes you can make to help improve your health and your mind. You can neglect one part of yourself and still expect to get the same results so remember to give all parts a try to get the best results possible.

It is our hope that you were able to get all the information you could need from this book and we hope that you will share your experiences with others. By reviewing this book not only will you be helping others with their decisions you will also being giving us invaluable feedback to help us keep improving any more information we try to provide in the future. Your feedback is so important to us and we value your opinion as our avid customer.

Here you will find the tools used by me!

New Article Submitter Software - Submit To 668 Directories! 

 Seopressor Wordpress SEO Plugin, Better, Faster, Higher Ranking!

Traffic Travis Free SEO And PPC Software 

 Backlink Beast - Best SEO Software

Made in the USA
Monee, IL
07 July 2026

56552451R00030